# Growing Pains

Mckenze Messman

Presentation by *BookLeaf Publishing*

Web: www.bookleafpub.com

E-mail: info@bookleafpub.com

ISBN: 9789357615747

First edition 2022

# remembrance

it's the first rain of fall,
and I still have dirt
under my fingernails
from when I knew
you last september.

I scraped my finger
on a vine,
and did not think of you.
I tripped and fell
in front of him,
and did not think of you.

but it's september
and it's raining,
and for the first time
in a long time,
I'm thinking of you.

# meditation

my blinds are missing
a fourth of the
thirty-fourth from the top
piece.
and it's not bothersome
or anything,
it doesn't keep me awake
during the day,
but I'll still stay up
late at night
and wonder
how it broke.

was there a cat who lived
here once?
who liked to stare out the window?
was it a grasping point for a
pair of lovers perhaps?
too busy with passion
to notice the damage they were
doing to the blinds,
that now belong to a
random young woman,
whose thoughts might
just linger too long.

# freefall

I don't know why
but I still think about
my old roommate,
who used to play
his guitar for me
when I was down.
I would listen to
the music he could
create with just his
fingertips, and some string
and I think it saved me.

I still hum along to the melodies
he played in the morning while I made
my coffee and
in the afternoon
while I tried to sleep.
I hope he's doing
well,
I hope he's still making
music.
I hope he knows I still have
his songs stuck in my head.

# quarantine

I'm at my best in isolation,
alone, without
someone watching me
and waiting.

when I'm alone I can
sing, I can
scream,
I can yell.

I can finally get angry about the
things I've been saving
for myself,
and I can fucking
cope.

# golden

you tuck my hair behind my
ear even though
we both know
it'll escape again,
and for a moment
I dream.

your thumb slides
it's way across my
cheekbone,
and you make it feel so
divine, I start to hope.

and then you kiss
that spot between
my thighs,
the one you know so well.
I open my mouth and start
to pray.

# vermilion

there's a chill lingering in the air
and I want to
lay down in it,
stretch out on a soft bed of leaves,
and sigh out my summer.

I want to watch the flowers
die off without morbidity
and without fear,
because I know
we'll see each other again.

I'd like to take comfort in this change,
I'd like to be a person who
can be okay with something
like that.
but I'll weep at
the first sight of orange,
and again when the first
of the leaves give up,
and I'll fall.

# ecosystems

Beelzebub sends his flies
to remind me that I'm
still somewhat human,
despite my years of
decomposition
and molding.
they bite at my ankles
and swarm around my ears,
I cannot block out the buzzing.

some other kind of god
sends his spiders.
they're in my house,
my hair, my shoes.
they're here to remind me to
be kind, I think.
to stop and collect,
just for a second.

# things I need to try for the first time:

oysters, surfing, walking with no destination in mind in a place I don't know, learning how to do something, and being alright with failure. ice fishing on a lake in Nebraska, speaking without thinking, and singing out loud in a crowd of people. ranch, letting things die off, letting things live. staying up all night to watch the sun set, and then watch it rise again. I need to swim with the dolphins, I need to learn how to pace myself, and how to talk in a room full of people without wanting to claw out my own throat. blackberry sorbet, planting wildflowers in a park, giving a note to a stranger just to see them smile, eco printing, writing from my soul, cliff diving at a tropical place, and living life without fear.

# spring

what am I here for if
not for the dirt
if not for the
worms if not for the bees.
what am I here for
if not for the
wind.
to feel it dancing across my skin.

# disappearance

I lost my grace the
day I grew my resolve.
the day I knew I needed boundaries,
and a spine,
she left me.

I found my peace shortly after,
in those moments when I
stood tall.

and though I miss her,
and ponder at the thought
that she may come back,
I know I can do without her.

# drought

I need to cry,
I need to sob until
the thunderstorm rages around me,
and weep until the ground floods up
to reflect my tears.

I need to scream so loud the
lightning startles
and dances with me,
but I can't.

like the sky my emotions are
dry, and every time
I find myself taking the time
to collect,
the tears never come.

# ellipsis

I'm trying my hardest
to not fall for you,
I'm grasping tightly
to every corner of my
being.
fighting with myself
every time I see the
brown in your
eyes.

is this naivety?
those three words are on
the tip of my tongue,
and I swear,
I'll bite it off before I let
you ruin me
with your sweet poison.

# tuesday mornings

and if I could rip the
world apart
and sew it back together
with just my fingertips,
to save these moments
for us.
the ones where
it's just
  me and you
I would.

# things I can't write about:

him. her. the way they both hurt me differently, and the way I thought it would never happen again. how scared I am that I'm not all the way healed from it all. how scared I am to live, how terrified I am that it'll all work out. the sun and the way they rays shine through the window, mid-afternoon. the way I want my words to mean something, but not just for me. my father, how it hurts to talk about him. the way I stare too long at the food I want to eat, before I eat it. how I don't know where I came from or how I got to be this way. how sometimes I feel like a stranger in my own skin, in my own shoes, and how sometimes I wake up in the middle of the day and I don't know how I got to where I am.

# frozen

I take a deep breath
every time I feel myself
slip away,
out of my body,
and down that little
river that I found that
one Saturday in march.

I can't describe what it's like but
I can feel it like a thorn
in my paw,
a knot in my side,
and a knife in my gut.

I hope I don't disappear again,
because I seem to do it every
time I'm with someone who
matters, and
I try so hard to be present that
it doesn't seem to matter anymore.
I keep slipping away.

# meadow

I was unlucky
to be born a girl.
how blissful would it be to
be a sunflower.
a peony, a wildflower.
waving gracefully in the grass
just waiting
for the bumblebees and
humming birds,
without a thought or care.

I could grow, I could
reach towards the sky
and no one would touch me.

except some lucky lovers someday,
wondering through my meadow.

oh to be picked, for someone's love.

# calla Lilly

you forget to water your plants
for a day
or two
or three
and all of a sudden they're
scorched from
the sun.

don't do that to me.
don't leave me
to wilt slowly from
your inattentiveness,
wondering when
I'll get my next drink.

I could grow flowers for you
if given a
touch of love.

# hello october

my love, you smell of
mulled cider and
spiced plums.
you taste of
sea salt and
hot chocolate.
and I used to shudder into
fall,
despair when the days
grew shorter.
but for you
my dear,
I will crawl into
bed with you,
under a warm blanket
night after night.

# manifestations

one day you'll
wake up and find that
you've grown into yourself.
your hair will be a half inch
shorter and
your smile will settle
into your face
just right.

you'll be driving halfway
to work before realizing
this is your routine now,
and it's not that bad.

you'll have people beside you
that you're petrified to
lose, and
they will look at you
like you are the sun.

you'll be scared every single day
that this is all just a dream,
but I promise you, honey
it's not.

# rationalizations

and I could black you out
of my heart and my mind,
like a poem
out of a book.
I could convince myself I
don't need you,
tell myself
I don't love you,
but who would be better off?

# prayer

say my name again
let it drip down your
throat like hot honey,
and swallow it with a promise.

repeat it like a prayer
get used to how it tastes
on your lips,
and grow addicted to
the way it feels caressing your tongue.

gaze upon me one more time,
so I can feel your eyes
and your smile
like a sunny day in November.

www.ingramcontent.com/pod-product-compliance
Lightning Source LLC
Chambersburg PA
CBHW070737160726
48003CB00006BA/2556